WHAT ARE COMMUNITY RESOURCES?

LEEANN BLANKENSHIP

Britannica®
Educational Publishing

IN ASSOCIATION WITH

ROSEN
EDUCATIONAL SERVICES

Published in 2018 by Britannica Educational Publishing (a trademark of Encyclopædia Britannica, Inc.) in association with The Rosen Publishing Group, Inc.
29 East 21st Street, New York, NY 10010

Distributed exclusively by Rosen Publishing.
To see additional Britannica Educational Publishing titles, go to rosenpublishing.com.

First Edition

Britannica Educational Publishing
J.E. Luebering: Executive Director, Core Editorial
Mary Rose McCudden: Editor, Britannica Student Encyclopedia

Rosen Publishing
Heather Moore Niver: Editor
Nelson Sá: Art Director
Matt Cauli: Designer
Cindy Reiman: Photography Manager
Heather Moore Niver: Photo Researcher

Library of Congress Cataloging-in-Publication Data
Names: Blankenship, LeeAnn, author.
Title: What are community resources? / LeeAnn Blankenship.
Description: First edition. | New York, NY : Britannica Educational Publishing, 2018. | Series: Let's find out! Communities | Includes bibliographical references and index.
Identifiers: LCCN 2016058549| ISBN 9781680487190 (library bound : alk. paper) | ISBN 9781680487176 (pbk. : alk. paper) | ISBN 9781680487183 (6-pack : alk. paper)
Subjects: LCSH: Communities—Economic aspects—Juvenile literatuare. | Natural resources—Juvenile literature.
Classification: LCC HM756 .B555 2018 | DDC 307—dc23
LC record available at https://lccn.loc.gov/2016058549

Manufactured in the United States of America

Photo credits: Cover, p. 1, interior pages (background) X Reflex/Shutterstock.com; p. 4 Rawpixel/iStock/Thinkstock; p. 5 Liderina/iStock/Thinkstock; pp. 6, 29 DragonImages/iStock/Thinkstock; p. 7 Comstock Images/Stockbyte/Thinkstock; p. 8 oporkka/iStock/Thinkstock; p. 9 LuckyBusiness/iStock/Thinkstock; p. 10 Nick White/DigitalVision/Thinkstock; p. 11 EVAfotografie/iStock/Thinkstock; p. 12 venturecx/iStock/Thinkstock; p. 13 Pixeljoy/Shutterstock.com; p. 14 Hermansyah28/iStock/Thinkstock; p. 15 PhotoMelon/iStock/Thinkstock; p. 16 Didacta_produktionsbyra/iStock/Thinkstock; p. 17 DimaBerkut/iStock/Thinkstock; p. 18 Tigergallery/Shutterstock.com; p. 19 Paul Matthew Photography/Shutterstock.com; p. 20 kajornyot wildlife photography/Shutterstock.com; p. 21 Aisyaqilumaranas/Shutterstock.com; p. 22 gbh007/iStock/Thinkstock; p. 23 sgtphoto/iStock/Thinkstock; p. 24 Laszlo66/Shutterstock.com; p. 25 Purestock/Thinkstock; p. 26 michaeljung/iStock/Thinkstock; p. 27 g-stockstudio/iStock/Thinkstock; p. 28 Rawpixel.com/Shutterstock.com.

Contents

WHERE WE FEEL AT HOME

Community resources are things that help meet the wants and needs of the community members. They can include the people of the community, goods and services, and natural resources.

The most important part of a community is the people who are in it. Community members might live near each other, be close in age, or speak the same language. No matter what they have in common, people in a community find trust and others who care about them.

In a community, people find others who are like themselves in one or more ways.

4

A mechanic uses his training, knowledge, and skills to provide a valuable service to the community.

Goods are items you can touch, like food, clothing, and furniture. They are either grown or made from raw materials.

Services are actions that people do for someone else. Services include delivering mail, repairing cars, and teaching classes.

Natural resources are things found in nature that people can use. Natural resources can be used to make other things, or they can be enjoyed on their own.

VOCABULARY

Raw materials are basic substances that can be made into something new and useful.

Caring for the Community

Goods and services are often bought in the same community where they are created. Sometimes, they are sold or exchanged with people in other communities. Either way, wealth is created.

Wealth is all things that have value when they are exchanged. The greater a community's wealth, the more it can offer its members.

When wealth is created, people have more money. Then, they can buy food or other goods and services they need.

The people in a community are also a kind of resource. A community might not have its own police or fire department, hospital, or airport.

Community members know their work is valuable. Helping one another makes the bond between them stronger.

COMPARE AND CONTRAST

Imagine that you and your family live fifty miles (eighty kilometers) from anyone else. How would your life still be the same as it is now? How would it be different?

But it could still have caring people who help each other. For example, neighborhood communities will always be important for people like single parents and older adults. They often rely on help from others who live nearby.

RESOURCES AND PRODUCTION

The process of making goods and services is called production. There are three major factors in production.

The first is land. Land can mean the ground where a business is located. A business can be a large farm or a tiny workshop. Land also includes natural resources. Natural resources are all the things that nature gives us. All goods come from the land in one way or another.

The workers are the second factor of

Production depends on land and natural resources, like water, forests, air, and soil.

production. This includes their skills and knowledge about their jobs. Nothing can be created, sold, or used without people to make it happen.

The third part of production is capital. Capital is all the human-made resources that are used to make and provide the goods and services. Capital includes tools, factories, equipment, and offices.

Workers' skills and knowledge are needed to produce capital such as buildings.

THINK ABOUT IT

Choose three objects in your home. Can you figure out how each came from the land?

RICHES FROM THE EARTH

Our planet, Earth, gives us everything we need to live. Examples are soil, light, water, plants, animals, minerals, and air. These natural resources can be used as food, fuel, or clothing. Some are used as raw materials to make other things.

Some communities have many natural resources. They

Earth supplies natural resources, like fruits and vegetables that keep us healthy.

A sheep's wool is a raw material that can be used to make cloth.

THINK ABOUT IT

What are some natural resources you need to stay alive? What are some that are not necessary but that make your life better?

may have good land and plenty of water for farming. Other communities may have minerals that can be made into products. The products can be sold to bring in money for the community. Some places have areas of natural beauty where people in the community enjoy spending time. Other places do not have many natural resources. They struggle to have enough food to eat or to make products that they can sell.

Gifts that Keep On Giving

If your library book is due today, you might be able to renew it. Then you can read it again tomorrow. The same is true of some kinds of natural resources. They are called renewable. They can be replaced or used again. Plants and animals are renewable natural resources because they reproduce, or make more of their own kind. After crops

Corn is a renewable resource used for food and to make ethanol, a fuel.

like wheat and corn are grown and collected, more wheat and corn can be planted. The same is true for trees. They can be cut down and used to make furniture or houses. More trees can be planted to replace the ones that were cut down.

Sunlight, wind, geothermal (heat) energy, and biofuels are renewable, too. We can use them without worrying that they will run out. But like all resources, they still can be damaged or destroyed if misused or wasted.

These solar panels collect energy from the sun to be turned into electricity.

13

Hidden Treasures

Some natural resources are limited. There are only certain amounts of them in the earth. They are nonrenewable because they cannot be replaced once they are used. Rock, minerals, metals, and fossil fuels are all nonrenewable. Fossil fuels are natural substances made from the remains of plants and animals that lived millions of years ago. Natural gas, petroleum (oil), and coal are fossil fuels.

People use fossil fuels every day. They use them to heat buildings, make electricity, cook, and run

Coal is a fossil fuel used to create electricity in power plants.

Crayons are made from a petroleum product called paraffin wax.

machines. They use gasoline and plastic made from petroleum. Petroleum is also in crayons, cosmetics, tires, paper cups, candles, and thousands of other things.

THINK ABOUT IT

Every year, petroleum is used to make more than a trillion plastic bags. Many of the bags become trash that pollute our land and oceans. What could governments or businesses do that would reduce the amount of plastic bags that people use?

WONDERING ABOUT WATER

Water is a renewable resource. It renews itself through the water cycle. When liquid water in oceans, rivers, and lakes warms up, it turns into water vapor. Water vapor is an invisble gas that floats into the air. As it rises, it cools and becomes tiny droplets. These droplets form clouds. Later, they fall back to the ground as rain or snow. This cycle means water can be used over and over.

Through the water cycle, Earth's water is constantly being reused.

But not every community has access to good water. Many people have to dig wells to get water from deep underground. It takes a long time to replace that water through the water cycle. Some scientists say groundwater is not as renewable as we once thought. As the world population grows, water is becoming scarcer and more polluted.

Garbage that is thrown into freshwater sources and oceans can release poisons that harm wildlife and humans.

GUARDING OUR TREASURES

Communities need water and other natural resources. Sometimes, however, getting at those resources can cause problems. The process can harm the environment. Also, if nonrenewable resources are used up, they will be gone forever.

To access natural resources, people often dig or drill into the ground. The mines or wells they make can cause land to erode or wear away. They often leave behind piles of waste. Sometimes, oil is spilled that destroys wildlife.

When fossil fuels like coal and petroleum

This 2013 oil spill in Thailand destroyed wildlife and put humans at risk.

are burned, they release chemicals. This harms the air, water, and soil.

Clearing land for buildings or farms can wipe out forests. Animals then are forced to move from their homes. This and other human activity can cause whole groups of animals to become extinct, or to die out completely.

Construction can pollute the air by making harmful dust and releasing toxic fumes.

THINK ABOUT IT

April 22 is Earth Day, a day to help the environment. What are some things you might do where you live?

COMMUNITIES AND CONSERVATION

Communities all over the world have found ways to protect their natural resources. This is known as conservation.

Every year, the US state of Virginia hosts "Clean the Bay Day." Thousands of people participate in the event and clean trash from Chesapeake Bay and its shores.

In the province of Buriram, Thailand,

In Thailand, farmers hand-harvest rice to avoid disturbing sarus crane nests.

the sarus crane (a kind of bird) had died out because rice farmers there used pesticides and noisy tractors. Scientists brought some of the cranes from another country and released them in Buriram. The farmers helped the birds survive by parking their noisy tractors and switching to organic farming. Organic farming is a method of farming that does not use chemicals.

People throughout the world participate in recycling programs. People set aside glass, plastic, and paper. Instead of being thrown away, those things can be reused.

This sea horse sculpture is an example of artwork using recycled trash in a fun, new way.

VOCABULARY

Pesticides are chemicals used to destroy insects.

Getting from Here to There

Not all community resources are made by nature. Many are human-made. For example, some communities build transportation systems to help their members get around. Transportation is all the ways people move themselves and goods from one place to another.

Communities usually provide sidewalks and roads. They build bridges and tunnels to make transportation easier. They have railroads for trains and docks

Some communities provide bike trails to make riding safer.

Trains are one way to ship resources over long distances between communities.

for ships. Sometimes, they build airports, highways, and public systems like subways and bus systems.

A community's economy depends on transportation. Raw materials must be moved from where they are found to factories. Then, products must travel from factories to stores. Food, minerals, wood, and other natural resources often travel by truck, railroad, or ship. People use transportation to get to school and jobs.

THINK ABOUT IT

In the past month, what different ways have you used to travel from place to place?

OTHER RESOURCES

Most communities have basic services and equipment that keep the community operating well. Together, these are called the infrastructure. The infrastructure includes all the community's public buildings and roads. Public utilities are also part of the infrastructure.

In many communities, you will find schools, libraries, museums, banks, hospitals, and government buildings. Police and fire departments protect people and property. Dams and levees control water and flooding. Other

Many communities provide services like recycling and trash removal.

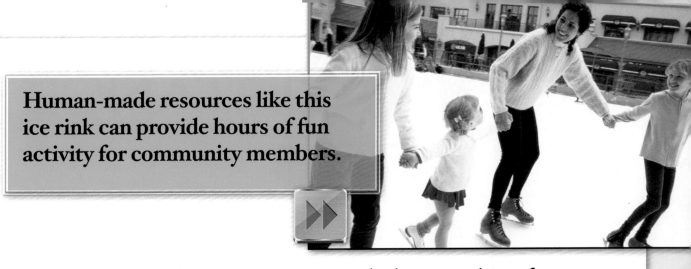

Human-made resources like this ice rink can provide hours of fun activity for community members.

human-made resources can include everything from loading docks and storage tanks to recycling centers and homeless shelters.

Some communities have park systems and recreation centers where people go to exercise, play sports, and have fun. Communities may provide walking and bike trails, soccer fields, and baseball diamonds. Some have tennis and basketball courts, swimming pools, playgrounds, and ice rinks.

> **VOCABULARY**
>
> A **public utility** is a business that provides a public service. Companies that provide natural gas and electricity to your home are examples of public utilities.

THE IMPORTANCE OF LABOR

People who work at jobs for pay make up the labor force, or human resources. They are another community resource or asset.

Each year in September, the United States honors workers with a holiday. Labor Day reminds us that the labor force helps improve lives in the community.

There are many kinds of jobs. For example, when you think about a factory, you might think first of workers who make the factory products. But there are also supervisors in

A quality control worker makes sure products meet customer requirements.

Planting trees is one way volunteers can improve communities and make them more beautiful.

charge of the work. Some workers repair the machines and check on safety, while others deliver the products once they are made. All the workers have special skills.

Men and women who do not have jobs that pay wages are an asset to the community as well. They care for their homes and families. Often they volunteer their time and talents to build and improve the community itself.

The Global Community

A community usually cannot make everything its members want or need. It might not have the right resources or enough people to do the work. To solve this problem, communities trade with each other.

Trade is the business of buying and selling items. Resources of all types can be traded. Those resources then can be used to make products that can be sold in other places. Improved transportation and advancements in

Technology like email and internet service has made trade and communication easier and faster than ever.

The wages from a paycheck might mean this young mother has money to buy fresh fruit for her family.

computer science have made trade between communities easier than ever.

Trade creates jobs. Jobs provide paychecks to the workers and their families. They then use their money to buy more goods and services. This cycle keeps a community's economy healthy.

COMPARE AND CONTRAST

List natural resources in your community. List some not found there. If you only had things on the first list, how would your life be the same? How would it be different?

Glossary

capital Human-made resources used in production.

conservation Planned protection, often of a natural resource.

environment All of the physical surroundings on Earth, including the air, water, soil, plants, and animals.

fossil fuels Natural substances made from the remains of plants and animals that lived millions of years ago.

geothermal Using the heat of Earth's interior.

groundwater Water found underground within cracks and spaces in soil, sand, and rock and that supplies wells and springs.

infrastructure A community's basic framework that includes all its public buildings, equipment, and services.

levee A bank built along a river to prevent flooding.

mineral A substance that occurs naturally and is usually obtained from the ground.

nonrenewable resource Something valuable found in nature that cannot be replaced once it is used up.

petroleum An oily flammable liquid obtained from wells drilled in the ground; the source of gasoline, kerosene, and fuel oil.

production The making of goods and services.

renewable resource Something valuable found in nature that can be replaced or grown back and used again.

trade The business of buying and selling items.

wealth All things that have value when they are exchanged.

FOR MORE INFORMATION

Books

Goodman, Polly. *Communities Today and Tomorrow.* New York, NY: Gareth Stevens Publishing, 2012.

Kalman, Bobbie. *What Is a Community? From A to Z.* New York, NY: Crabtree Publishing, 2000.

Kenney, Karen Latchana. *Economics Through Infographics.* Minneapolis, MN: Lerner Publications Company, 2015.

Loria, Laura. *What Are Resources?* New York, NY: Britannica Educational Publishing, 2017.

Ritchie, Scot. *Look Where We Live! A First Book of Community Building.* Toronto, ON: Kids Can Press, 2015.

Yasuda, Anita. *Explore Natural Resources.* White River Junction, VT: Nomad Press, 2014.

Websites

Because of the changing nature of internet links, Rosen Publishing has developed an online list of websites related to the subject of this book. This site is updated regularly. Please use this link to access the list:

http://www.rosenlinks.com/LFO/resources

INDEX